The Pocket Guide
To Fashion PR

Sophie Sheikh

GW00470210

First published in Great Britain in 2009
Reprinted 2009

ISBN 978-0-9561336-0-1

A CIP catalogue record for this book is available from The British Library

Printed in Great Britain by
the MPG Books Group, Bodmin and King's Lynn

With sincere thanks to Mark, Iram, Nas and Laura J London.

The Pocket Guide To Fashion PR

CONTENTS

The Pocket Guide To Fashion PR

Introduction

So what is The Pocket Guide To Fashion PR?

The Pocket Guide to Fashion PR contains a wealth of advice and insider information on the exciting and fast paced world of Public Relations.

Ideal for the new designer and some of the more established women's wear and accessory brands, this guide will focus on the core aspects of establishing and maintaining a fashion PR plan, whether on your own or within a team.

By concentrating solely on the world of fashion and the printed media, this guide is an introduction to the skills and dedication needed by any individual wanting to raise awareness, gain recognition and ultimately increase the sales of their product. From press releases to general emails, meetings to industry jargon, the guide cuts through years of training and takes you straight to the heart of fashion PR.

The guide is designed for those with minimal experience of Public Relations. It will enable you to keep PR activities close to home and under your purse strings, as well as providing invaluable tips for those already succeeding in their PR strategy. From maintaining press relations to securing coverage in national magazines and newspapers The Pocket Guide to Fashion PR gives you a chance to successfully compete against powerful public relation firms and more established brands.

What will fashion PR do for me?

In time you will reap many benefits from maintaining your own PR plan. They include:

- Increased sales with both new and existing customers

- Receiving acknowledgment and endorsements from your target media.

- Gaining the attention of potential stockist's such as independent boutiques and department stores.

- Gaining credibility and desirability when approaching financial backers.

- Assist you in attracting better staff who wish to work with a label such as yours.

- Increasing your chances of collaborations and cross marketing opportunities.

- Enable you to bargain with new and existing suppliers and manufacturers etc.

- Attract celebrity customers and endorsements

What if I don't have the time handle my own PR?

The Pocket Guide To Fashion PR does not expect full time dedication to your PR campaign. We recognise that you are already busy with the designing and manufacturing of your products while possibly even holding down another job to fund your dream. Once you have completed this guide, you will appreciate that structure and organisation will enable you to maintain your PR campaign in just a few hours each week.

What if I don't have the budget to maintain my own PR?

This guide is designed for those with a minimal budget for PR. If you have access to the internet, a phone, a computer and a camera then you are able to begin work on your PR campaign.

Can't I just place an advert rather than struggle to gain coverage via PR?

Of course! But what do you pay more attention to: the products endorsed by a fashion editor or the products that are lost in the back pages of a publication under the header *advertisements*? Anyone can buy an advert, but it's far harder to secure a valued endorsement from a figure of authority. Advertising may be the quicker route to exposure but it is not the most valued or respected.

Ultimately you have made an active choice to push your brand, open doors of opportunity and create a brand that will make its mark upon the industry. The Pocket Guide to Fashion PR will help you realise these goals and assist you up the first steps of the Public Relations ladder.

About the author

Sophie Sheikh is a fashion coach and founding director of Preo PR. Preo was born from a love of fashion and a desire to offer fledgling labels the opportunity to compete with the bigger industry names. Sophie's passion for the products has always been the driving force behind every successful campaign. From front page coverage on national broadsheets to online marketing opportunities, Sophie has been instrumental in the success of many of the UK's most exciting fashion labels. Sophie now acts as a coach and mentor to the fashion industry.

Keeping A Record

Record keeping is perhaps the most important aspect of handling your own PR. By retaining clear and concise records of your actions you will speed up the entire PR process as well as keeping confusion to a minimum.

When handling your own PR you must be sure to keep a record of every action you take. From the sending and receiving of your products to recent conversations, every PR step should be logged on to some form of sheet, computer document or diary. This is a valuable exercise that will ensure you stay on top of your Public Relations strategy and will keep confusion to a minimum.

We strongly suggest you organise your methods for record keeping before you commence any form of PR. We also advise that you form at least the skeleton of your press database before you move on to other areas of your PR campaign.

We have provided five basic templates to record details that we believe you should be keeping. You can tweak these as time progresses and perhaps morph several sheets into one.

(All names are fictitious)

No 1 – Press Database

As the name suggests, your press database comprises of all the applicable individuals from your target media list. It will be an ever evolving collection that you will update on a regular basis. In time, this database will be heaving with contacts but to begin with, focus on a just handful of publications. By examining your target press, you can make an informed decision on which individuals will be most suited to your collection. As your knowledge of the various publications grows, you will become familiar with specific names and pages. Soon, you will be sure of exactly who is an ideal press contact for you and your label.

For now, your database should include all members of the fashion department for each target publication. You can then choose to focus your attention on two or three individuals for the early stages of your PR plan. As suggested, if you commence with five publications (perhaps two monthlies, two newspapers and one website), then you will be opening doors of communication with around ten to fifteen people in the first leg of your PR strategy. Do decrease this number if it seems a little too daunting to begin with.

We always recommend that you maintain your press database on a reliable computer programme such as Microsoft Outlook. This template lists the basic details you will require for each individual contact. Should you prefer to use a hard copy press list, we suggest you categorise contacts into publications and list individuals in the order of job titles. E.g. Fashion Editor above Junior Fashion Editor.

TIP:
The credits page confirms the hierarchy of job titles, with the editor's name at the top of the list. Credit pages are can usually be found at the front of a publication, within the first few pages.

PRESS DATABASE

PUBLICATION
ADDRESS
SWITCHBOARD

NAME	TITLE	DIRECT LINE	EMAIL	FAX
NAME	TITLE	DIRECT LINE	EMAIL	FAX
NAME	TITLE	DIRECT LINE	EMAIL	FAX
NAME	TITLE	DIRECT LINE	EMAIL	FAX

PUBLICATION
ADDRESS
SWITCHBOARD

NAME	TITLE	DIRECT LINE	EMAIL	FAX
NAME	TITLE	DIRECT LINE	EMAIL	FAX
NAME	TITLE	DIRECT LINE	EMAIL	FAX
NAME	TITLE	DIRECT LINE	EMAIL	FAX

No 2 – Record of Press Communication

Telephone messages and emails may not instantly appear to be worthy of record. However a dozen such telephone calls, combined with customer and manufacturer enquiries could be tricky to recall by the end of a working day. That is why keeping a note of each conversation, email and meeting is so important. You need not write an essay for each entry, just a few bullet points featuring key points from each conversation will suffice. If for example a stylist informs you that they will be away for a two weeks, add this as a bullet point along with the best time to get back in contact with them.

The following template suggests how to maintain these notes as a hard copy. As a PR company we print off a new template for each month, even though we also update the information under the individuals contact details on the computer. This is because we are contacting press every day, it therefore makes sense that we have all our recent information in one place and ready to hand as it would waste time opening up specific files on the computer each time we wished to make a call or send an email. With a monthly hard copy, we can simply glance down to see who we should be checking in with and when.

PRESS CONTACT OCT'08

DATE	CONTACT	PUBLICATION	NOTES
2nd	Amber Levy	Marie Claire	Only shooting skirts, call in 3 wks
4th	Tom Alder	The Telegraph	Fab meeting, shooting gold shorts,
4th	Lisa Jayne	The Observer	on maternity till Feb 09, Claire Ale covering
5th	Sarah Lloyd	Vogue	Not calling in, requested press release,
5th	Grace Benjamin	OK!	Not calling in for three weeks - call then

TIP:
To aid the organisation of press correspondence and to appear more professional, set up an independent email account for your business, i.e. press@usual address.

No 3 – Press Samples, Sent and Received

Each time a piece from your collection is sent out to a press contact you must make a record of it. Should you leave a sample with a contact following a meeting, immediately make a note of the sample(s) and add them to the sheet below (or other chosen means of record) on your return. You will see there is space to include a description for each piece. This may be more useful to an in-house PR rather than to a designer who is more familiar with their own collection.

> TIP:
> In the description box it is also advisable to include the size you have sent, this will make stock checking easier for you.

These records are particularly useful to keep close to hand. Not only do we keep all these records on an excel sheet, we also keep a hard copy in what we call the "Sample Bible', an A4 folder packed with sheets similar to this template. Always within reaching distance, the bible enables us to quickly remind ourselves of a sample and lists the price should the recipient of the sample call us for the cost and stockist details. It always gives a better impression when you can offer required information immediately, rather than saying you will call them back with the details.

As you can see the template includes boxes to insert the dates on which the item was sent and returned. As time progresses and your turnover of press samples increases you may find it beneficial to organise these sheets into specific publications with the help of dividers, e.g. a sheet for Elle magazine, a sheet for The Times etc.

Press Samples - Sent & Received

CONTACT	PUBLICATION	PIECE/DESCRIPTION	£	Sent	Rtrnd
Tom Alderley	The Telegraph	Gold shorts 10	85	04-Oct	16-Oct
Nia Law	In Style	Blue wedge heels 38	129	06-Oct	21-Oct
Belinda Lee	Handbag.co.uk	Silver mermaid necklace	35	07-Oct	09-Oct
Sarah Lloyd	The Observer	Yellow & black clutch	110	08-Oct	16-Oct

No 4 – Dockets / Delivery Form

There are two types of dockets you will generally come across: those you receive and those you send. Your docket will be sent out each time you send products out to press. How your docket or *delivery form* looks is at this stage up to you, however it must consist of four key points:

- Your company details/where the delivery is from
- The name and publication of recipient
- The exact contents of the package with details if necessary
- The date on which the parcel was sent

Dockets that you receive from the press will be inside or attached to a delivery. They will include their company details and a list of the samples included in the package. Such packages are generally organised by a fashion assistant or intern.

> TIP:
> Temporarily store dockets you receive from press. They will be referred to in the event of a missing or damaged sample.

When sending out a docket create two copies and retain one for your records. Note the space to include images of the enclosed samples – we have found this to be an excellent method of limiting confusion for all parties. We saw an immediate decline in missing samples once we applied this feature to our delivery slips. As with all the templates we have provided, you will want to make changes that reflect the visuals of your brand.

Company Logo

FASHION DELIVERIES

Your company name, address, contact telephone numbers,
email and website addresses

TO: name of recipient   PUBLICATION: name and address

FROM: your company details   DATE: date delivery is sent

List the products that are included in the package, specifying the style,
quantity and colour. E.g.

Quantity	Description
1	Black cord trousers with gold piping 12
1	White shirt with black buttons 10
1	Black wrap dresses with yellow trim 10
2	Gold and silver wedges, size 38

Total Samples: 5   Signed _____

You can
include images
of the enclosed
products

Somewhere on the docket you can clearly state what your terms are should any
of the samples enclosed be lost or broken. E.g. *"Should the enclosed samples
be lost or damaged by PUBLICATION, YOUR BRAND will invoice
PUBLICATION for the wholesale price including VAT".*

No 5 – Forthcoming Press Coverage

In theory, you should never forget when you are expecting press coverage, however in practise such events can slip your mind. Keep this sheet in a prominent place and update it as new press coverage is confirmed. We always update our hard copy sheets with forthcoming press dates and we also add them to a white board. If you have the room in your studio or office, this will be a wise investment and will soon become a fixture that is checked regularly by you and your team.

TIP:
Should you miss any of your press coverage, you can always order a back copy. Many publications have a back copy department. Simply call the switchboard and they will put you through to the correct person.

FORTHCOMING PRESS COVERAGE

PUBLICATION	CONTACT	DESCRIPTION OF COVERAGE	ISSUE
The Telegraph	Tome Alder	Gold shorts, most wanted feature	October
In Style	Natasha Law	Blue Wedges, main fashion shoot	January
The Observer	Sarah Lloyd	Yellow/black clutch, hot shop	Dec 2nd
Elle	Polly Brown	Green velvet belt	TBC

Release Yourself

We will regularly refer to your press release throughout this guide. Your press release is simply a few paragraphs providing key points on you, your label and your current collection.

You may wish to produce new press releases for individual developments throughout the season. However, for this chapter we will be working on a one off press release that will be used for the duration of one season.

A carefully written, strategically sent press release should successfully relay your key messages. It should be an easy to read summary of your offerings for the season and will encapsulate the elements that make your new collection so enticing.

The Story

A popular method for writing press releases is to concentrate on the 5 W's. To ensure these W's are applicable to the fashion industry, we have provided you with the following points to consider:

- **Who?** Brief description of the label/designers, who you are
- **What?** What products you design and for what season
- **Why?** Why you have been inspired, why you design
- **Where?** Where to find the collection; shows or stockists
- **When?** When the collection launches, when it is available

The idea is to then answer these five questions in the opening lines of your press release. You then elaborate on these points within the subsequent paragraphs. You may find there is a crossover of subjects covered within each 'W', so you should be able to combine various answers within a few paragraphs.

Once you have completed the first draft of your press release, we suggest putting it to one side for a short time. Over thinking the process can lead to frustrating writers block, so have a break before you return to edit. When you are ready, read through the draft and begin to remove the superlatives. Words such as 'fabulous' or 'brilliant' are not considered necessary unless they are in the form of a quote from an outside party. Success words however, are another matter. Some words act as instant attention grabbers. Examples include 'event', 'best-selling' 'launch' and 'award-winning'. Similarly, throwing in a few big names to a fashion press release will also demand some attention. For example 'McQueen' and 'Westwood' are immediately familiar, so if you have previous experience of working with any big names, be sure to include them on your press release.

Continue to edit your text until you are happy with the results. If possible, ask a friend or colleague to read the press release and provide an honest critique. The average press release should consist of around 200 words. Some of you may struggle to reach this figure, whilst others may battle to bring the word count down. Fear not, in time you will settle in to a tone of writing that makes composing you press release an easier process. The first few attempts will always be a steep learning curve. Take a look at other examples of press releases. Be inspired by other labels and their approach to this PR tool.

TIP:
Why not have a mini stockist list at the bottom of the page, or perhaps details of any forthcoming events and/or exhibitions.

Visuals

At the end of this chapter you will find examples for the layout of a press release. Although you can be creative when designing your own press release for the fashion arena, there are a set of professional guidelines that you must stick to. They include:

- **A4 sheet, one side**
  Upper limit of 200 words

- **Contact information**
  Ideally printed letterhead paper. Clearly specify who press should contact for additional information. Website address, telephone no's and emails etc

- **Clear heading**
  Must specify that it is a Press Release and clearly state the season. Usually the brand name & title of the collection

- **2" margin**
  Leaving a 2"/4 cm margin for editing notes

- **Double spacing**
  Easier on the eye and looks neater

- **Clear Font**
  Italics can be unfriendly on the eye

As you will see, our press releases include images. If for some reason the press release is unaccompanied by a lookbook, then the reader will still be able to make an informed opinion on your collection.

1"margin   1"

LOGO
www.
PRESS RELEASE

AUTUMN/WINTER 2007

IMAGE	IMAGE	IMAGE

SHORT SUMMARY OF BRAND (The 5 W's)

Paragraph 1: About you and your label - **Who**

Paragraph 2: Inspirations, materials etc - **What**

Paragraph 3: Your key message, target customer - **Why**

Paragraph 4: Any key stockists/fans/celebs etc - **Where**

Suitable quotes from buyers etc. And/or forthcoming
events/shows - **When**

Paragraph 5: For more information please
contact… website and email

Key Stockist's: additional stockist can be included on
a separate page if necessary

CONTACT DETAILS

LOGO

PRESS RELEASE

AUTUMN WINTER 2007

SHORT SUMMARY OF BRAND **(The 5 W's)**

IMAGE   Paragraph 1: About you and your label - **Who**

Paragraph 2: Inspirations, materials etc -**What**   IMAGE

Paragraph 3: Your key message, target customer - **Why**

IMAGE   Paragraph 4: Any key stockists, fans, Celebrity fans etc - **Where**

Suitable quotes from buyers etc. And/or forthcoming events/shows - **When**   IMAGE

Paragraph 5: For more information please contact…website and email

CONTACT DETAILS

Knowing The Names

When contacting your key press you should possess at least their basic information, including their full name and job title. This chapter offers suggestions for obtaining and maintaining a solid contacts database for your target media.

Before you commence regular contact with your target press, you must possess the following details for each individual listed in your press database:

- Their full name
- Their correct job title
- Their direct telephone number and/or switchboard number
- Their email address
- The address of their respective publication

Obtaining all the above information in one sweep may be difficult unless you have access to an existing database. It is more likely you will build up a collection of details on individuals as you progress. Unequivocally, never get in touch with a member of the press without knowing their name and job title at the very least.

There are a number of ways to locate the contact details for your target press, some are more costly than others. Here are a few examples.

Subscription Services

There are fashion related companies whose main focus is to maintain a press database on your behalf. Fashion Monitor and Diary D are two such services. Generally offering their customers several packages, you can choose the level of subscription you feel best suits your requirements. You may be able to purchase a one off catalogue of contacts (a collection that will need updating manually as the seasons progress). Or you can subscribe to an annual service that will inform you of any press movements, name changes, promotions, or retirements. Such subscriptions may also keep you abreast of the latest fashion news and developments which can also be extremely useful. Which ever service you decide to subscribe to, you will almost certainly come to find it invaluable.

The Credit Pages

You can locate a list of editors, assistants and more in the credit's page of any publication. The credit's page is a directory of all the individuals involved with the issue, ranging from Feature's Assistant to Art Director. The list is in order of importance, thus the Editor's name will always be found toward the top. Although not always titled 'Credits', this list can be found within the first few pages and occasionally elsewhere within a publication.

Do be aware that most monthly magazines are prepared several months in advance of actual publication so there is ample time for job titles and employees to change. The individuals who helped create the June issue of a monthly publication may have moved on by the time the issue comes to print in September but they will still be listed in the credits.

Take care in noting subtle changes in job title. It can be easy to miss the promotion of "Acting Deputy Editor" to "Deputy Editor". Consider your frustration if you were continually referred to as an assistant when you had been promoted to Manager some time ago. Always make immediate changes to your database if a contact has recently married and taken a new surname.

If in doubt, check a name and job title with the applicable switchboard before making contact with a stylist, editor or journalist.

Websites

Another method of obtaining names and job titles is to visit the publication's own website. Many of these sites now feature a directory of their employees under the "contact us" pages. If the directory does not include a list of individuals working for the hard copy version of the publication, it may at least list all those involved with the website.

Throughout your PR campaign you should be continually refreshing your knowledge of all target publications and contacts via any correspondence you have with them.

To Give and Receive

This chapter relates to the sending and receiving of products to and from your target media. We discuss how to present your products and what information should be included each time you send out press samples.

Much of your allotted 'PR time' will be spent dealing with the turnaround of press samples. The sending and receiving of products to your target media is time consuming but a vital aspect of a PR plan.

Sending

If you are London based and sending samples out on a regular basis, it is advisable to open an account with a recommended courier firm to access their cheaper rates. Courier firms may appear to be a costly option but is making a quick call to place a booking more beneficial to you than queuing in the post office or delivering the package yourself?

TIP:
If a publication contacts you to request samples, ask them if they are able to send a courier to pick up the products. If they say no, simply send your parcel as normal.

Ultimately how you send your products will be a direct reflection on your label. Think carefully about your packaging. Would you rather the press received a plain plastic bag with samples apparently thrown in, or might they prefer to receive a logo printed bag with products carefully wrapped in coloured paper? Such packaging efforts need not cost the earth. As mentioned at various points throughout this guide, your computer can be one of your greatest allies. A few carefully designed A5 stickers can work as wonderful logo carriers for the front of your bags. Coloured tissue paper casing each sample will send the message that your products are important to you and should be treated with care.

Ensure your products clearly exhibit your brand name. As discussed in the chapter "Keeping a Record", we include a docket in every delivery we send out. We also add a short hand written note to the recipient with any applicable press releases or additional information.

> TIP:
> Remember, each label, sticker and docket is free advertising for your brand. You are raising awareness of your label every time you send out a delivery.

When sending samples out to press, ensure the following actions have been completed:

- Parcel is clearly labeled with the name and address of the recipient

- Parcel is safe and secure, products inside are protected

- Parcel reflects a positive image of your brand

- Parcel includes all samples requested by the recipient

- Parcel includes a docket and note for recipient, clearly specifying how to return the products

- Each enclosed sample exhibits your brand name

- Parcel includes any suitable additional information, e.g. press release, lookbook, biography etc

<u>Coming In</u>

Consider this: you have made five calls to the fashion cupboards of various magazines, all to chase samples that you awaiting. All five fashion assistants assure you that the samples will be returned by courier the following day. The next morning you cancel your lunch appointment and wait patiently for the returns. By 3pm only one bike has called for you and by 6pm you are still expecting four separate packages.

Unfortunately, if you have guaranteed that you will be in the studio/office, then there you must stay. Press departments have to justify and pay for all their couriers, so they won't take kindly to having to re-send products because you popped out. It can suggest a lack of professionalism and neglects the silent promise you made to be reliable and consistent. It could deter them from using you again.

> TIP:
> Publications with the same address (under the same publishing company) will often use the same couriers to make deliveries. When applicable, combine the returns by letting each magazine/newspaper know that a courier from their building is already coming your way.

One solution is to specify a specific time for couriers to arrive. E.g. before 1pm. This is no guarantee but it will be in everybody's interest to adhere to this timeline and is often a successful method when organising the return of your products.

Another option is to clearly state on all dockets - and via related calls or emails - that returns should be made via Registered Post through Royal Mail. This ensures that rather than samples being returned to the magazine (sent to the dark abyss that is the post room), they will be safely held by your local Sorting Office.

Another option is to arrange returns yourself. Unless you have an unemployed friend who enjoys collecting parcels, this option can be more costly as it relies upon you paying for your own delivery service to pick samples up from press. All the fashion departments would need to do is prepare your parcel as normal and leave it with reception or internal post room. This method means you are in total control of the sending and returning of your samples, however it will mean extracting slightly more information from the press in your initial call. For example, you will need to know when you can send a courier, where the courier should pick up from, etc.

Also worth considering, is the possibility of hiring a company whose sole job is to sign for deliveries. Many such companies are London based and for a fee will accept and sign for all courier deliveries on your behalf. They can then forward these parcels on to your specified address or prepare the parcels for you to pick up yourself. Although costly, these services are particularly useful if you are based outside of London, work from home or do not feel your postcode reflects your brand appropriately.

Looking Good

This chapter is concerned with the shooting, presentation
and desired effects of your images.   From lookbooks to
j'pegs we discuss many of the options open to when handling
the visual side of your PR plan. We also provide advise for
preparing for a shoot.

Good images are a must for any fashion label and they are the
greatest vehicle for exposing your label. The styling, the model and
even the location should transmit a positive message of you and
your brand.

When you have successfully shot and produced the images, you
will organise them in to what is known as a 'lookbook': a
collection of images from your collection that will be used to entice
customers, press and potential stockists.

There are various options when deciding how to shoot your
collection, here are just a few:

- A studio shoot with professional model
- A studio shoot with mannequin
- Location shoot with model
- Still life shoot with white background
- Still life shoot on location

We prefer to shoot products against a white background.   Busier
backdrops can often distract from the products themselves.

Aim to include each piece from your collection. If you design throughout the season, you may prefer to use a mannequin or opt for the still life option. Recreating an orchestrated shoot for additional pieces later on in the season may be tricky. Ensure you can update these new pieces easily in to your lookbook as they arrive. Here are examples of the style of images you can feature in your lookbook.

Model shot, on location

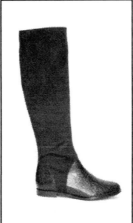

Still life image, on white background

Model shot with white background

Images supplied by Philmore Clague and Laura J London

It can be tempting to cut corners with shoots, for example using a friend as a model or taking some quick snaps up against your office wall. Remember these images will be sent out as the direct reflection of your label and must send a professional message as well as successfully exhibiting the designs themselves. As with every aspect of this industry, vision and message is key.

Unless you are able to conduct the entire shoot yourself, you will be looking for individuals that will assist you when creating your lookbook. If your budget does not allow for experienced professionals then entertain working with new talents who have not yet made their mark. You work in a sector that is brimming with enthusiastic new cadets, eager to gain experience and widen their portfolios, take advantage of it.

- Quiz friends and colleagues for recommendations

- Visit web sites that showcase the talent you are looking for

- Contact model agencies – they often provide new faces for lower rates than their established names

- Approach photography agencies – they too may wish to promote a new client for reduced fees

- Contact desired venues – they may want to raise their profile by holding fashion shoots for no cost

- Approach students - inexperienced but passionate and trained

This is also a perfect opportunity to establish long term relationships with new talent that may help your label as you both continue to grow.

TIP:
Press may request that you email images of your products. 300dpi (dots per inch) is generally the minimum resolution a publication can run with. As a general rule, press require sharp and focused images that will sit well on their pages and complement the other products. When including images in general emails, reduce the size of an image to approximately 120 dpi.

Until your financial budget for exposure is brimming, it is likely you will be using the same set of images when sending information to press, buyers and individual customers. You will probably want to feature the images on your website as well. In this case, the pictures really do need to exhibit as much information as possible.

For example, if you have featured a blue bag, list all other available colours. It can also be useful to detail the materials and textiles you have used. Another vital detail to include with each image is the price. Remember the fashion press work with retail prices only, buyers require wholesale prices, so it is a good idea to include the costs as an insert to a lookbook. This allows you to add the relevant price list for the applicable recipient. To make things easier, number images to tally up with the related price (as in our examples). That way press and buyers can simply glance at the insert to discover a price.

The layout and packaging of your images relies heavily on your budget. A professional lookbook created by a design and printing team is generally quite costly, so perhaps you can create a few ideas of your own, taking inspiration from existing lookbooks and catalogues. Remember, there is no one template with lookbooks and something different will always stand out from the crowd. That said you must adhere to a vague set of guidelines that include:

- Exhibiting high quality images
- To successfully reflect your brand
- To include all company and contact details

A fashion stylist can receive several hundred images from various labels each week so ensuring yours is eye catching and unique will always keep you one step ahead.

As the quality of printers and inks improve, it is becoming easier to create professional lookbooks on your own computer. As a designer it is likely you already have a keen eye for detail and even without relevant experience, you may find you prefer your own creations to that of the professionals.

Keeping lookbook design and even printing in-house ensures you can keep all information up to date at the touch of a button. Furthermore you are not left with any unused lookbooks at the end of each season. This option is also useful if you continue to design throughout a season as opposed to producing two strict collections each year. You can simply update the images as and when new pieces arrive.

Care and consideration is key and time will be spent on each and every aspect of design, from the layout of the content right through to the card you print on to. Undoubtedly more budget friendly, this option is far more time costly and over seasons you may prefer to outsource this responsibility to the professionals. However for your first few seasons at least, it will be an effective tool that will broaden your experience and familiarise you with a fundamental aspect or your PR campaign.

The Shoot

Should you decide to run with a full on studio shoot, the following text will be of use to you.

Larger shoots require more planning and it is advisable you have a clear agenda for the days' events. You would be surprised to discover how many shoots fail to complete successfully as the designer has forgotten to bring along a signature dress or an emergency iron. Ensuring the following actions have been taken will help the day run smoothly.

- If you are working with a photographer/make up artist/stylist/model, ensure you meet with them before the big day to discuss your goals, the theme and general break down of the day

- Organise in advance the pieces you will be shooting. Style the outfits if necessary and write up the order in which you want the samples to be shot

- If you are paying a photographer you will usually be charged a set day rate. Although this means you are in no urgent hurry, it does mean a re-shoot on another day will cost you. Make sure you have a timeline of what you need shot and when. Allow for more time when shooting a more complicated piece

- If you are shooting on location, visit the site before the big day and note a few key areas to shoot in or around. Where applicable check that there will not be any coinciding events such as road works or festivals

- In the week leading up to the shoot, create a check list of all the items you will need, adding to it as the week progresses

- Confirm transport arrangements to and from the venue for the products and the participants

- Confirm in writing the fees for each participant

- On the day itself, ensure you have enough provisions to prevent various participants popping out every half an hour for drinks or snacks (however unless agreed otherwise, staff are entitled to a lunch break)

- Check images with your photographer as you go, assessing whether or not you are achieving the desired look

- Always ensure all samples are clean and ironed or steamed. It can be a good idea to take along a steamer or iron (if there are plug sockets)

Most of all, enjoy the day. Play music and keep anxiety to a minimum. If all parties are clear on the goals then the results should be as you had imagined. Photo shoots can be great fun and are often memorable experiences. They remind you that other people are also passionate about your label and are a great way of establishing long term relationships with like minded professionals.

TIP:
If possible, take advantage of the facilities, have a mini make over and take a few professional shots of you and your team. You may be required to provide these images for future press coverage.

I Just Called

Confidence and preparation is key when calling your target press. 'I Just Called' discusses many of the situations you will need to deal with when dealing with press contacts over the phone. It covers the messages you need to send and receive and provides several examples of typical press/designer conversations.

Calling the press can be a daunting experience but in time your confidence will grow. Much of your time will be spent talking to press over the phone, so it is crucial that you become accustomed to the practice early on in your PR plan. As we have previously suggested, begin the process with just a handful of individuals to contact and tailor your conversation to their particular needs.

If you have prepared the monthly press sheet to keep track of your press communication then you should find it easy to retain clear records of all your conversations with target press. When dealing with any individual in the media, remember:

The best person to sell your collection is you. In theory there is no question you can not answer and no area of your business you are unfamiliar with.

Before you begin your calls for the first time, take a moment to relax. Make a note of the points you wish to cover in bullet form and refer to them throughout the conversation. Compose your thoughts and remind yourself of your key objectives. They are:

- To open doors of communication with an individual

- To send a positive message about you and your label

- To receive information that will benefit your relationship

- To send and receive information that will lead to exposure

Unless already acquainted with the individuals in question, you are effectively cold calling. This is not to say that you are bothering them. Until a stylist suggests otherwise, you are of interest to them. It is their job to discover new talent as well as showcase the established, so they should always be interested to hear about genuinely exciting or original new labels.

At certain times of the week or month (depending on the publication), fashion departments will meet to discuss and decide what themes and styles they will be working to for the forthcoming issues. The fashion pages may reflect the theme of the entire publication, such as a Christmas issue or summer special, or they may focus on the latest fashion week. Ultimately they will know what they want to achieve and what they require to achieve it. Once the meeting is over, they will set about calling in appropriate samples.

For most main fashion shoots, stylists will work to a break down. A break down is an internal brief, generally consisting of the following information:

- The main theme (any influences/era's they are reflecting)

- The products they require

- The colour scheme they are working to

- Who is styling the shoot

- Where and when the shoot will be taking place

It is your job to discover the best times to contact your target press, making sure your calls or emails coincide with the days they are calling in. Of course there will be occasions when you contact them outside these times and be successful in achieving press coverage but knowing the best times to call and email press will always work in your favour.

The first call to any contact should be a polite introductory conversation telling them who you are and what you do. Don't take up too much of their time, simply offer to send them information and confirm how best to send it. If you happen to catch them when they are looking for products, do suggest sending over a sample if you think it is suitable but don't push too hard or you could damage the relationship. The key messages you want to send and receive in this <u>first</u> call are:

- Who you are

- The name of your label and the products you design

- Your price points

- Any key stockists/department stores/online boutiques

- How best to send them information on your label

There are a number of turns the conversation could take from here. You might find the contact takes an immediate interest in your label and is eager to see images or samples themselves. Perhaps they seem disinterested and you end the call feeling a little rejected.

Either way, unless they have requested you do not contact them (which is highly unlikely), you have opened the doors of communication and made them aware of you and your label.

From here on, your main goal when contacting your target media will be to gain press coverage. You might find it takes time to receive a printed endorsement from any publication but your motivation and desire to achieve this must not waver.

Ultimately your goal is for the fashion press to see, touch and perhaps even wear your products. You need to ensure that your samples are close to hand whenever they are shooting and that you are aware of any shoots that your samples could be suitable for. The easiest way to achieve this is to ask them.

When you next call a contact, remind them of who you are and exchange niceties. You then need to ascertain if they are currently working on any features, shoots or pages that your collection could be involved with. When contacting press there are several lines you can use to entice their interest. We have provided a few suggestions, along with possible responses. As with all our templates, you can alter them to suit your style.

Quote 1

"......just checking in to see if you need any jewellery/accessory samples over the next week or two..."

Simple and straight to the point, this sentence requires a fairly simple response. If they do require such samples, make an exact note of their requirements and let them know what you will be sending and when. See check list of related questions at the end of this chapter. If they do not require samples such as yours, ask when would be the most suitable time to call them again. If appropriate, offer to re-send information on your label.

You might find the contact claims to be unfamiliar with your label. In this instance, refresh their memory, tell them a little bit about your collection and politely remind them of the information you have previously sent them.

> TIP:
> Jewellery and accessory designers – make sure you contact the Accessories Editor of a publication (if applicable). They are most likely to take an active interest in your collection.

In the event of not having any suitable samples, try not to make a negative statement such as "we don't have anything like that". Simply say that if you have anything suitable you will send it over, then arrange a time to next contact them.

> TIP:
> Jewellery and accessory designers are often able to create new pieces with short notice. If you feel you could create a bespoke piece befitting a press request then go for it. It won't guarantee you press coverage but it will impress the contact and send a clear message that you want your label to succeed.

Quote 2

"...we have a great new selection of three inch wedges..."

"New" is a buzzword when dealing with the press and they like to offer their readers the first on a new line. Ideal for gaining coverage in shopping pages and still life features, this statement tells the contact exactly what you have and can often lead to last minute press coverage to complete a page in their publication.

If your *something new* reflects the current trend then it is even more effective. Familiarise yourself with current and future trends and become a regular visitor on fashion forecasting sites. Take inspiration from successful catwalk shows and tally strong themes up with your own suitable pieces. As a designer, it is likely that this is currently part of your routine anyway, so simply translate your knowledge in to PR talk. If you know pencil skirts will be big news next season, then push your own new range of pencil skirts whenever suitable.

Quote 3

"...recently been taken on by a department store"

Never underestimate the power of a new stockist. Ultimately, this is on some level, newsworthy, particularly if the boutique in question is well known. By buying in your label, a stockist has exhibited faith in your creations and even if no samples are sent to press via this particular conversation, volunteering this information helps the stylist make an informed opinion about your label. With enough stockists, press will soon follow suit and appreciate that your label really does have something new and exciting to offer.

Quote 4

"....I have previously worked with..."

There is a thin line between dignified self promotion and blatant name dropping, however the fashion industry can sometimes be a who-you-know business. It can aid your cause to mention a high profile fashion house or design team you have worked with. If key industry figures have placed trust in you, the press are more likely to take an active interest in your label.

Question's Check List

If a contact has requested samples, there are a number of questions you should ask before sending the samples out. They include:

- When do you need samples?
- Is it still life or will you be using models?
- What sizes do you need?
- When is the shoot?
- Where is the shoot?
- Where shall we send the samples?
- When will the samples be returned?
- What issue is it for?
- Will it be credited?
  (applicable to advertorials and celebrity shoots)
- Do you need single or pairs?
  (applicable to shoe call in's only)

In time you will not need to ask so many questions as you will be familiar with the way a particular fashion department works and to what speed. Soon enough, dealing with press over the phone will be second nature. Your confidence will grow and introductions that are carefully considered when you first begin, will roll off your tongue with ease in just a few weeks.

> TIP:
> If you encounter a new contact during these initial press calls, aim to obtain their contact details. Then offer to send the information on your label.

Meeting Of Minds

Before long your PR plan will involve meeting press contacts face to face. This can often be a daunting aspect of the PR process however any fears must be conquered to establish successful long term relationships with your target press.

Professional friendships can be established over the phone or via emails but no other form of communication is as effective as a face to face meeting.

Unless you have access to a showroom or suitable venue to hold a press viewing, consider taking your samples to the publication. Fashion press will often spend entire afternoon's visiting various PR companies and showrooms to view collections, so offering to take your designs to them will save them valuable time and exhibit your eagerness and willing.

Key advantages to taking your collection to them include:

- One to one time with a key press contact

- An opportunity to relay more information than is possible via an email or telephone conversation

- Sending the message that this individual is important to you, their feedback is valued and you are keen for their attention

- You are not competing with other labels in a conventional showroom environment

- You will have a privileged insight in to the mechanics and general feel of a publication – particularly if you are meeting in the fashion department itself

- You have sufficient time to explain each label as you go, something that is not possible via the medium of lookbooks or random j'pegs

There are of course specific times to exhibit/introduce new seasonal collections but don't feel confined to the industry's protocol. Rather than compete against large PR firms for press attention at peak times, you might find success lies in arranging appointments mid season. Such timing is particularly suitable to those of you who design and produce throughout the season and regularly have new pieces to show.

From a ten minute viewing in the reception to an hour's lunch appointment, spending time with your target press will contribute greatly to the success of your label. By knowing and understanding you the designer, target press will do the same for your collection.

Of course, it's not like booking a dentist appointment. Press meetings are in high demand and tricky to secure. Most of us in the PR industry continually *need* appointments and if it were so easy to borrow twenty minutes of a journalist's time, then we would all be in deep discussions with editors or stylists. It may take many calls and emails before a key contact agrees to meet with you, however as with every aspect of PR, securing press appointments will get easier the more established your label becomes.

When securing press appointments, remain flexible with your time. Consider the press's other commitments such as deadlines, shoots, and castings. Continually busy, your target press may change dates and times at any moment, so be prepared to work around their schedules. It may be an inconvenience for your calendar but your efforts – and understanding - will undoubtedly pay off.

Now you have secured your press appointment, you must prepare for it. Refresh your knowledge of the stylist in question. Take another look at their pages, remind yourself of the publications target reader and their price brackets. By tailoring the samples you take to their individual requirements, you are sure to gain a more positive response and reap more benefits from your limited time.

> **TIP:**
> If possible, ask the contact you are meeting if they wish to see any particular samples. It is unlikely you will be taking your entire collection, so check what they are working on and take samples that may work with a specific issue and/or theme.

Be sure to prepare your signature pieces as well as samples that work with the relevant season. For example, if you are meeting a junior fashion editor of a monthly publication in March, note that they will be focusing heavily on products to suit the May to August issues. Ensure all products are packaged appealingly, this will relay a good impression when you unveil them during the meeting.

Gather your press releases, biographies and any lookbooks or images you will be leaving with the contact. Be sure to pack a notepad and pen (you may need to make notes soon after or even during the meeting) and unless you know them off by heart, do take a product price list.

> **TIP:**
> Take several copies of the above literature. You can never be sure of who you might bump in to and it is always worth taking duplicate information in case you should meet a fresh contact.

Once you have secured one press appointment, why not contact additional publications that are within close proximity. If you are in town with your samples, maximize your time and try to arrange additional appointments before you set off. This is particularly pertinent if you are coming in to London especially for press appointments. In such instances, you may find it beneficial to take an extended trip in to the capital for at least a couple of days. If you find yourself regularly having meetings with press, it may be worth while investing in a wheelie case for clothing or a travel bag for accessories.

There are several venues in which your appointment might be held, ranging from the publications reception to an official meeting room. The decision on the venue will usually be outside of your control. Many of the major magazine's and broadsheets occupy one floor of a London based building, with sister publications within the same building. For example Elle and Red magazine are both based at 64 North Row whilst Vogue and Tatler are both based in Vogue House. Each publication usually has their own reception area and it is not uncommon to take press through your samples in this space. Although it can be cramped, it is a great way of catching passing trade (i.e. other press), so do keep your eye out for familiar faces.

TIP:
Some publications feature photographs of their staff, either in the first few pages or aside the stylist/journalist's article. These are a great way of familiarising yourself with names and faces, ideal when waiting in the reception area.

Depending on availability, you may find yourself in one of the publications' official meeting rooms. This means more room in which to exhibit but less chance of bumping in to useful contacts.

The use of *bumping in to* might sound optimistic but some PR is born from luck alone and you can't afford to miss an opportunity. Other possible venues include the in-house café or restaurant, at the journalist's desk (which can be cluttered but very insightful), or even on location of an impending shoot.

> **TIP:**
> For the appropriate label, always wear your designs to a press appointment. Not only is it free advertising, you must be seen to be endorsing your own designs.

During the meeting, try not to rush. Maximize your time by focusing on key points and allow the journalist time to ask questions and make comments. Every bit of feedback you receive will give you a greater insight into their needs so listen carefully and try not to overload them with your information.

You might find the journalist wants to take sample(s) from you there and then. In this instance make a note of what is borrowed and be sure to log it in your press folder when you return to the office.

Aim to discover the stories and trends for forthcoming issues, features and shoots. It is unlikely you will have this much exclusive time with a key contact over the phone so use it wisely. Also take the time to enquire about your journalist's needs. Ask at what time of the week or month he or she prefers to be contacted or when the general editorial/fashion deadline of the issue is.

Knowing if he or she prefers emails to hard copy lookbooks can make a huge difference to your future correspondence with them. By gathering this information during all your meetings, your understanding of individual press will grow, leading to more successful relationships with your target writers and stylists. Once the meeting has come to an end, be sure to leave with them all the literature and imagery you prepared earlier. Arrange a casual time to contact them again and thank them for their time.

At some point over the next few days, drop the journalist an email to thank them once more. Omitting such courtesies can negatively effect the impression you leave on a journalist and after all your work in actually securing the appointment, you don't want to blow it all by not rounding things off appropriately. You want this meeting to be the first of many, not the first and last.

At this point, it should be worth noting that you have not just secured yourself a new best friend. Just because you have spent an exclusive half hour with them, it does not mean that you and your journalist will now embark on a sample filled relationship, seeing each other every month. You have made the first step and presented you and your label to a specific magazine and a contact within. You have opened the doors of communication and hopefully started a successful professional relationship. Do not now over contact the journalist, as to expect automatic coverage from them would be unrealistic. Connect with them only when you need to, or when they have asked you to.

If you are arranging an appointment with a freelance stylist, the above pattern will be almost identical however you will likely meet in a less formal location such as a coffee house or studio. Don't hesitate in asking to move the venue if you feel the atmosphere might damage your samples.

MEETINGS CHECKLIST

- Confirm a date and time but be prepared to change it

- Find out what stories they are working on before the meeting, prepare suitable samples and signature pieces

- Refresh your knowledge of the applicable magazine, target reader, price points and when appropriate, specific pages

- Gather any images and literature you wish to leave with the journalist. Ensure you take several copies

- Pack a note pad and pen

- Pack a product price list

- Contact other journalists that are within close proximity to your meeting. Aim to secure more than one appointment on the same day

- Leave doors of communication open on your departure

- Be sure to thank the individual for their time within the forty eight hours following the meeting (excluding Fridays)

A Week In The Life

The following chapter provides you with an idea of what your new working week might look like if you embark on maintaining your own PR plan. It highlights how you can integrate PR activities in to your existing timetable, without jeopardising your current commitments.

In time you will settle upon your own timetable in which to maintain your PR plan. Finding time for PR activities may be a struggle but it is vital you prepare at least a vague agenda for your week. Having clear weekly goals will aide you both in the long and short term. Successful PR relies greatly on organisation and planning as well as making time for any unexpected enquiries.

TIP:
Never bite off more than you can chew when maintaining your PR plan. You can always extend your target press list however it will be tricky to minimise it once you have already opened doors of communication. Turning your back on press contacts may jeopardise your long term relationship with them.

It is vital that you remain on top of any outstanding PR tasks and dedicate time to generating new ones. Consistance is key in Public Relations and your plan will suffer if you dip in and out of your duties from one week to the next. Some tasks will vary from week to week but calls must be made, emails must be sent and press releases must be posted. Taking your eye off the ball for just a few weeks will lead to missed opportunities and you may lose the interest of your target press.

What follows is a basic example of one week in the life of a designer who handles their own PR, illustrating how a PR plan would be integrated in to the working week. In time you will settle in to a regime that suits you.

Mon 3rd	- Expecting delivery of new silk for dresses 10am-12pm
- 2PM:	Meeting head buyer for Stone boutique – Charles cafe
- 4-5.30	Print off new copies of press releases and biogs for the week,
	Check phone and email messages for press enquiries
Tue 4th	- post designs off to the manufacturer
10-12pm	Call target press contacts: chase returns/see what they are working on. Confirm Fridays appointment with Clare.
12.30	Lunch with Kay jewellery designer to discuss collaboration
2pm	General designing and pre production
Wed 5th	Send info to TBC and On:Off for consideration to show
10-2	General designing etc go through CV's for work exp
2 – 3	Deal with any press enquiries, update website with new press
3 – 6	General office work/designing etc
Thur 6th	Go to newsagent – new monthly publications should be in
10-11.30	Make any outstanding press calls from Tuesday. Check all requested press releases and lookbooks have been sent.
	Ensure all records are up to date.
12-6	General office duties/designing etc
Fri 7th	*Pick up Daily Mail *send Elle dress * Call Eve @ Red
10-10.15	Check emails . heard back from the Telegraph?
11-12	Meeting with accountant,
1.30	Appointment with Clare @ The Times

Going Online

Many of you will consider launching a website or online boutique. 'Going Online' discusses many of the issues involved in this aspect of your business and includes an exclusive interview with the founder of the successful footwear boutique www.lollipoplondon.com.

Recent studies show that internet fashion expenditure has risen by over 500% in the last six years. Most of the established brands have an online presence and it would seem that to attract that elusive international market, one must be prepared to consider selling online.

I use the word consider, as no business should be forced in to making a decision that could potentially damage the entire progress of the brand. With so many considerations when launching an ecommerce sit, time and money must be budgeted carefully. If such resources could be better spent elsewhere, then do not move too quickly in to the online arena.

There are of course advantages and disadvantages to launching an online boutique. Effectively you have gained a new international boutique and are now able to continually update customers on all your developments. However, new issues will arise such as threats to security or faults with your server. Such issues will invariably act as new distractions for your working day.

> **TIP:**
> Retailing your products via another online boutique will give you access to the online customer, without the hassle and worry of launching your own ecommerce site. You can then direct your customers towards this website.

Fortunately there is now a multitude of information for the budding online retailer. For many customers, online shopping is fast becoming as popular as its' physical counterpart and as the years pass, new generations of shoppers will consider shopping online the absolute norm. Courses, books and websites dedicated to retailing online seem to have sparked a mass movement towards this relatively new phenomenon. You are even able to find ready made websites, fully equipped with the ecommerce facilities.

An extension of your brand, your site is simply another vehicle through which to relay your message. The reaction to your site should be close to the reaction a customer has when they walk through the doors to your boutique. Each product you display online should be accompanied by a description. Ultimately you are compensating for the missing sense of touch that ecommerce subtracts from the fashion buying process, therefore you must give the customer every reason to trust in your "virtual" product. Similar to purchasing from a catalogue, the customer can never be completely sure of a product until it has arrived, so you must simplify the process and build a level of trust between the site and the customers. This can be achieved a number of ways:

- **Good description:** A few words on the texture, fit and any additional helpful advice

- **Strong visuals**: Featuring perhaps two or three different angles with close ups on key details

- **Moving Website**: Alternating home page visuals (but not entirely changing the look of the site) and ensuring new continually updating will keep the site fresh and live

- **Clear terms & conditions, delivery & returns policy**: Ensure customers can clearly check and understand the terms & conditions, delivery and returns policy along with any incurred costs

- **Packaging:** Describe your packaging if possible include an image of a packaged product

- **Press Page**: Once you achieve press coverage, make sure a copy is loaded on to your site asap, endorsements by publications can be a great way of instilling trust in the customer

Press Coverage for your website

As the gap between the 'online' and 'real' shopping world slims, so too do the differences between the potential methods of press coverage you can hope to achieve.

Treat online press coverage in the same way you do the hardcopy publications. You will already know that all the best publications (including all of the newspapers) have their own online presence, many of them offering an almost exact replica of their printed format. Monthly glossy publications tend to provide a more diluted version of the current issue and some even work as their own entity – covering different topics, featuring their own fashion spreads and articles. Elleuk.com and Marieclaire.co.uk are great examples of such sites. They clearly possess the same passion for fashion and news as their printed sisters but are able to maintain an independent take on the industry as a whole.

Online fashion departments are as keen to feature your products as their hard copy relatives. It could be said that your chances of achieving press coverage are greater thanks to their quick turnover and need to keep their readers interested. Features such as 'Buy of the Day' (Marieclaire.co.uk) demand a quick turnover of new information in the fashion office so the appropriate editors and writers will be keen to see new products that you have to offer.

Such pieces of press coverage will usually provide a direct link to the specific product on your website, so only submit a product that will definitely be online and available to buy when the coverage transpires.

> TIP:
> As with all press coverage, aim to compare the number of visitors to the site just before and just after a piece of press coverage comes out.

You will also be aware of the countless internet shopping directories that appear in the hard copy publications. Many established fashion pages now dedicate entire pages to online shopping and they are always keen to hear about new sites. Ensure that the appropriate editors and stylists are aware of your new site. Whether you host a launch party or decide to work quietly through the opening few months (assessing and addressing any teething problems) before contacting press, your target media must be made aware of your website within the first season of launching. As with all press coverage, features, mentions and references will not come to you – it is your job to seek them out.

> TIP:
> Once your site is up and running aim to include your website address in all future pieces of press coverage.

Interview

Launched in 2005, the Laura J shoe boutique (previously known as Lollipop London) gained international acclaim thanks to a vast array of impressive press coverage. Two years later, founder Laura Allnatt felt it was time to launch the online boutique. Over a year in the planning, the website successfully launched mid 2007.

Why did you decide to launch the website?

"We knew there were shoe lovers around the world who were desperate for footwear that was different to the products available on the high street. Launching our online boutique enabled us to turn Laura J in to a global brand and it has attracted new shoe lovers who might never have discovered us"

What were your initial fears?

Cost. Outgoings can spiral when launching a website so we were always concerned with staying within budget. It was important to us that our site was deemed 'trustworthy' and the decision to accept an off the shelf payment form (e.g. paypal) or a bespoke process was an issue. In the end, we opted for a bespoke process.

What were the hardest and most worrying aspects to the design and launch of the site?

Again, cost. I can't stress enough how much time and attention must be paid to the budget throughout the entire process. Also, deciding on what aspects of the site we could realistically keep fresh. We were extremely keen for our site to reflect a minimal yet continually moving impression but it was difficult deciding exactly what aspects we would be able to stay on top of. You also worry that all the time and money will pay for itself long term. Building and launching a site is one thing, its success is another.

How do you react to the online competition from other shoe retailers?

We are extremely conscious of our competitors and regularly asses positioning, marketing strategies and listings. There are many ways of staying ahead of the pack, some you obviously need to pay for. Google ad words have worked brilliantly for us.

What has been your best moment since launching the site?

The day of the launch and our first online sale.

What has been the greatest surprise?

Probably the incredible press reaction we have received, combined with the customer feedback which has been so positive. It really inspires us.

Can you give one key selling point of your site?

Each pair of shoes is shot from multiple angles so customers can appreciate the entire design. Shoes are our business so it pays to ensure the products are as clearly displayed as possible.

What do you consider to be the positive benefits of the site?

Now we have launched the online boutique, new doors have opened up to us for promotion and we are gaining even more excellent press coverage. A great site can reflect a great business, regardless of the actual size of your team or premises. This will undoubtedly invite new business along the way. Lastly, a solid site makes launching a new product to both customers and industry a much easier process.

What advice would you offer to a label or boutique wanting to launch their own website?

- *Create a striking brand*

- *Dedicate part of the budget to marketing*

- *Keep the site fresh and updated to attract regular customers*

- *Be clear on how you handle sales, deliveries etc*

- *Provide thoughtful packaging that sends a positive message*

- *Never send out an order until their payment has cleared*

- *Send out regular newsletters to notify customers of stock, offers and news*

- *Stay on top of the possibility of fraudulent purchases. Ideally take on an online authorization company for all transactions*

Show Off

In time you may wish to partake in a fashion show or exhibition. 'Show Off' is dedicated to the process of exhibiting your designs and discusses many of the options that are available to you.

Soon enough you will exhibit your collection. You may partake in an established event, or choose to organise an exhibition of your own. It is likely your exhibition will coincide with fashion week, (give or take a few weeks) and it will be necessary for you to do at least some profile raising to attract visitors.

Depending on the nature of the exhibition, your target guests will range from existing and potential customers, to press contacts and even boutique owners and buyers.

Established, non-official fashion week events are gaining kudos with each new season. On : Off in London is one such event. Attracting the fashion stars of tomorrow, many of On : Off's exhibitors move swiftly in to the official London Fashion Week tents within a few seasons. Understandably designers need to have attained a certain level of success before such events will allow them to participate.

TIP:
There are a growing number of events that run outside peak "fashion week" times. Such exhibitions are held in venues around the UK and can often attract a great number of press and buyers. Examples include Pure and Boutique London.

Alternatively many new and established designers choose to secure their own venue (either alone or with a collective) and host their own "off-schedule" event. From a one off catwalk show to a static exhibition, such events can last from one afternoon to an entire week. Many designers choose to hire a hotel room to host a static open house exhibition, whilst others rent a space for a one off catwalk show. Ultimately the choice of venue will decide upon the messages the label wishes to send, the ambience they wish to create and of course, their budget.

The larger, established events will have official organisers to generate PR; inviting suitable guests and attempting to secure press coverage that will benefit the exhibitors. Self planning an event will require you to generate your own PR.

Most exhibitions – established or otherwise - will carry a financial cost. From a set fee, to a percentage of sales, exhibiting is not a cheap option, particularly around fashion week's, when venue's are in demand. However, an event can be judged a success by just one outstanding order, so executing your event plan correctly can be one of the most important projects of the season.

Inviting The Press

London Fashion Week is the busiest time of the season for this industry. Not only must the fashion pack squeeze in all the "must see shows", so too must they meet and mingle, impress and be impressed.

With this in mind, it would seem that an event featuring a new collective of five or so designers will not be as high on their agenda as an official re-launch of a big name designer. This is not to say you will not receive the odd editor or stylist but be aware that bigger labels will have bigger turnouts to their events, thus taking potential guests away from your own function.

TIP:
Whether showing alone or within a collective, choosing a venue close to the established LFW tents will increase your press attendance. Make the geography work for you.

More exhibitors at an event can be more of a temptation for the busy fashion pack. Should you exhibit alongside ten other labels, you will no doubt receive a greater turn out than the event hosted by just three labels. Once again, put yourselves in their shoes. With deadlines, appointments and the minimum one hour delay which appears to haunt Fashion weeks, time is tight. Expecting a stylist to travel even slightly off their carefully planned agenda can be asking too much. So offer them an excellent reason to take time out of their schedule to attend your event.

TIP:
Choose your fellow exhibitors wisely, particularly if you are parting with money. Mismatched unions of designs can have a negative impact on both the aesthetics of the event and the guest attendance.

Select your guests wisely. Treat your guest list as you do your general target press list. Don't add names or publications for the sake of it, bumping up numbers with irrelevant guests could come back to haunt you. Imagine if the advertising executive of a low shelf women's magazine keeps you in such deep conversation, that you end up missing a vital introduction with a stylist from one of your more preferable publications.

TIP:
Adding texture with friends and family is great for moral support but be sure to spread their attendance over the duration of the event.

Always keep a list of those invited and subtly cross off names as guests arrive, perhaps note any main points of conversation. Such tasks will help you establish an excellent database and allow for quick reference when looking back on the success of your events.

An Inviting Proposal

Although you will no doubt be sending reminders and confirmations via email and perhaps telephone calls, the invitation itself is what will offer the first impression of your event.

January, February, August and September are the busiest months for the sending and receiving of invitations within the UK's fashion circuit. An attractive invitation will always hold more temptation than an email or photo copied print out so try to encapsulate the mood of the show in the invitation.

> TIP:
> Recall the photo shoot for your collection. How did you translate the brands' qualities through still life images? Draw on these initial influences when designing your invitation.

If you are showing alongside a group of designers try to unite a common theme. Perhaps all work on one idea, then draw out the strongest elements of each to use for the ultimate invitation.

> TIP:
> Your first few events are a great opportunity to build new relationships with the assistants at a desired publication. Targeting the new generations of fashion press can lead to extremely fruitful, long term associations.

As with every 'outbound vehicle' for exposure, ensure you have investigated the market and compared your ideas with the tried and tested. Consider other invitations you have seen for similar events, appreciate your likes and dislikes from them.

Remember that a hand written note accompanying an invitation will always demand more attention that one without. To save time, why not draw up a short list of the most important invitees and be sure to include this note with their invitations.

> TIP:
> Fashion Weeks are international events. Why not open up your target media list to include international individuals or publications that you have not previously contacted.

As with all contact with press, ensure you have the correct spellings, job titles and addresses before sending out any invitations. If applicable, follow up a week or so later with a call or email to confirm the invite arrived safely. Individual emails would be ideal however if this is not plausible then perhaps send out a newsletter reminding everyone of the date, venue and exhibitors. It can be hugely worthwhile stating that "invitations can be resent if required".

Preparation is Key

Preparing for your event is key. Of course you will have a checklist for all the collection-related aspects of the event, such as order forms, swing tags etc, however do not neglect your check list for the PR aspects of the event. Here is a basic checklist. Quantities of each must be considered before you leave the office or studio.

- Press Release

- Lookbooks/images

- Biography

- Price lists (retail and or wholesale where applicable)

- Swatches (where applicable)

- Stockist List

- Business Card

- Forthcoming event listing

Press Pack

Many of the sheets listed can be organised in to what is known as a 'Press Pack'. The format of your press pack will probably remain consistent throughout the season and should theoretically be suitable to send out to press, customers and buyers, long after the show.

You can contain the press pack in a folder (A5 size is often most convenient for all recipients), or an envelope. Creativity is key but do note that loose sheets and random pages are not ideal. The packaging and colours should adhere to a standard theme, this can be most easily achieved by using your brand logo on each page. The press pack will allow you to swiftly offer visitors a round up of your label, even if they choose not to stop and speak with you. It is advisable that you leave a collection of press packs on a nearby table or alongside your collection for passing guest to pick up should they desire.

Packaging each press pack may take some time if you opt to design and package yourself but make sure you are armed with a sufficient amount for the event. Any left over packs can easily be sent out after the show has run.

Gifts

Depending on the nature of your brand and your budget, you may wish to include some kind of gift within your press pack.

One option is a money-off voucher to use against a purchase from your collection. You can design and produce your own, stating how much of a reduction the voucher represents. Anywhere from 15% should be generous enough. Vouchers can secure residency on a fashion desk or pin board for some time after the event – all subconscious brand awareness. And of course there is the possibility of a future sale and new relationship.

Speaking with the press

Often this will be the first time you meet many of your target press contacts. Securing private appointments with press can be difficult so Fashion Week is a great opportunity to put faces to names and formally introduce yourself.

If you have chosen to partake in an established event, then it is likely the event organisers will expect attendees to wear a name badge, stating their company/publication and job title. This is useful when trying to distinguish press from other disciplines.

Unfortunately, disguising such details is far easier for guests at a smaller event. Key contacts can slip in and out without conversing at all with the designer/hosts.

This is where remaining alert and open to subtle hints is key. In this industry, you can never be sure of who is in the room. The most understated woman in the room might easily be the fashion editor of a high end publication.

> **TIP:**
> Many magazines now feature images of their fashion staff alongside features. If possible, gem up on faces before any event, particularly those you have invited.

Most of us dislike being seized upon by representatives, so always allow people their personal space. However if someone is taking a clear interest in your collection, then don't shy away from introducing yourself. Always allow someone time to explore a few pieces then casually open up a conversation without making them feel they must commit to your exchange. If you find the individual in question is not open to communication, then why not offer them a press pack. A closed question, that shows willing, without invading their space.

When you find yourself dealing with a press contact, offer them the press pack and express your genuine interest in their publication (this is where your knowledge of publications comes in to its own). As with all press communication, do not overload them with information. Appear calm but keen and casually arrange a suitable time to contact them post Fashion Week.

Following up

Following any such event, indulge in some well earned time off to refresh and reflect. Now would be an ideal time to make notes. How do you feel the event went? Could you have done anything better or differently? What changes do you want to make before you next exhibit?

Once the madness of Fashion Week has subsided, you can begin thanking your guests. A newsletter can be a great way of sending your thanks to all attendees however do take the time to individually thank key contacts (press, buyers or customers) who you felt made a specific and valuable contribution.

Now is also the time to get in contact with any press contacts you were fortunate enough to have had a one to one with. Do bear in mind that you were just one of many labels they saw over Fashion Week so don't take offence if they need reminding of you and your label.

> TIP:
> Be aware of the fashion packs diary. Just because London Fashion week is over, check when other fashion weeks such as New York or Paris begin.

Don't forget to add new contacts to your database and update any news and information on existing ones. Every event you visit or partake in is a great opportunity to expand your database.

Going It Alone

If you choose to organise or participate in an event that is not being coordinated by professional organisers, here are some of the aspects that will need to be considered:

Location
Must be easily accessible and ideally close to existing fashion week attractions

Access
Ensure you can drop off/pick up products easily

Power Supply
Confirm you have access to an electricity supply if necessary. If you are organising a catwalk show that will include lighting and effects, you might want to secure a technician for the event

Heating/Ventilation/Air Conditioning
Depending on the season, do check the room temperature will be suitable for all participants

Toilets
Confirm they will be available to guests as well as exhibitors

Kitchen
If you will be providing a food or drinks, you may require a kitchen to prepare in

Cleaning
Confirm who will be cleaning/tidying the venue of completion of the event

Going It Alone - Additional considerations:

- Insurance	- Staff	- Sound/entertainment
- Lighting	- Security	- Photography/Video
- Theme	- Decorations	- Disabled Facilities

Do's and Don'ts when Exhibiting

DO:	DON'T:
- Establish relationships with fellow exhibitors	- Leave anything until the last minute
- Wear your own products (when appropriate)	- Allow visitors to take any samples away with them
- Consider enlarging and exhibiting images of key pieces	- Let your space become messy. Tuck bags and coats out of sight
- Consider a theme if you have your own stand	- See fellow exhibitors as competition.
- Bring a notepad & pen	- Be late or leave early
- Bring provisions	- Look bored or disinterested
- Offer a strong, enthusiastic handshake	- Overload guests with too much information
- Consider hiring a model to wear your products	- Leave the stand unattended unless unavoidable
- Have an emergency kitty	- Bring strong smelling food
- Be aware of body language some people may not want to be approached	- Underestimate the power of press coverage. Exhibit key coverage clearly
- Take a chair and table (if space allows)	- Tire of repeating yourself. Keep conversation fresh
- Smile and have fun!	- Let boredom get you down

Loose Buttons

At some point a button will fall off your PR plan and invariably you will have to deal with damaged samples, lost accessories and frustrating obstacles that might hold you up. This chapter reveals some of the black holes you will encounter and how best to approach them, as well as offering a few pointers for other, more general aspects of handling your own PR.

Lost /Damaged Samples

In the event of a fashion department losing one of your samples, there are a number of options open to you. Firstly you could invoice the publication for the wholesale or retail amount of the sample, including VAT if applicable. Before invoicing, consider your relationship with the particular publication. Have you had any press coverage through them? Are they showing a keen interest in your label? You will need to respond to missing sample cases individually. Invoicing a magazine could jeopardise your future relationship.

An alternative option is to try and gain coverage as compensation for the loss. Rather than insisting that they repay the cost of the product, ask if there are any shoots or stories coming up that you might be suitable for. No need to spell it out but offer them an olive branch that benefits you. They may have mislaid or damaged one of your samples but you could gain some priceless press coverage in return.

You can always choose to forgive and forget. However you might find your samples have a habit of disappearing because there is no reaction by you or your team when products are not returned.

Deliveries and returns have plenty of opportunity to go missing and in our experience it is usually a genuine mistake. However the way you approach the situation can affect future relations with target press so always weigh up the importance of the sample and the relationship.

TIP:
Always check your products as soon as they arrive from press. If you notice any damage to the samples, flag it up immediately. Check the small print on the docket, some publications will only handle queries within a specific time.

Clearly borrowed

Although rare, there have been a few occasions when samples have clearly been worn. If you have loaned out samples for a main fashion shoot it is likely they would have been worn outside and you can expect slight wear and tear. For this reason it is always a good idea to have one press sample of each design from your collection, this way, you are not out of pocket if the sample becomes so worn it can not be sold to a paying customer. If however, a sample is returned so weathered it can not even be used for another press shoot then you must aim to seek the compensation described in the Lost/Damaged samples section.

Mis-prints

If one of your samples is used in a fashion shoot, then it is vital that you are credited correctly for your designs. However there are occasions when publications print inaccurate information. In this instance, you must notify them immediately. No publication wants to provide their readers with incorrect information and they will usually do all they can to rectify the situation.

The publication can notify readers of their mistake in a subsequent issue or, as with missing samples they can provide more coverage as a means of apology. The important point to remember in this instance is that you are losing potential sales and possibly giving another label credit for your designs. Be sure to persevere when seeking an amendment.

No Show

Someone from a publication - typically a fashion assistant - will notify you of forthcoming press coverage within their publication. This call is usually combined with a request for the product's price and a telephone number to provide to their readers. However this call is not a guarantee of coverage, no matter how assured the caller sounds. With so many departments involved when finalising an issue, there is always a chance your feature or product will be dropped at the last minute.

Before despairing over a no show, call or email your contact to enquire if your feature has been officially dropped or simply moved to an alternative issue.

Coping with rejection

JK Rowling approached over ten publishing companies before the Harry Potter series was finally accepted for publication. Even the Beatles were rejected by record companies before they discovered success. Rejection is a process everyone experiences at one time or another, so learning how to deal with it and move on quickly is vital to your success.

For each fan there will be a critic waiting in the wings, for every testament to your ingenuity and forward thinking, there will be a slight on your talent and an accusation of rehashing a past style.

The well known saying is entirely true – you can't please all the people all the time. However do not brush off all criticism as occasionally such feedback can be constructive. If it suggested your designs are poorly finished for example, do consider if there is a touch of truth there. Could you move your production to a slicker manufacturer?

To a degree, fashion stylists, editors and assistants will always adhere to dictated trends born from the catwalk, but they work in this industry because they have a passion for fashion and no two minds will think alike. So, if you walk away from one meeting with a heavy heart because the other party clearly did not take to your creations, simply book another meeting and appreciate that the next stylist could love your collection. As clichéd as it sounds, keep your head up and don't let a few random negatives get you down or hold you back.

Dry Patches

It is common for a designer to feel as though they should be gaining more press coverage than they are. Likewise, when press coverage is achieved, it is easy to presume your label should feature in all the magazines all of the time. Whatever your status in the industry, dry patches will occur. Certainly, the more press you gain, the more press will inevitably come your way but presuming you deserve coverage is dangerous ground.

As a designer and sales person you should believe your product will be a success. If you work hard on your Public Relations plan then undoubtedly you will realise a level of success. But, you must not presume that one piece of coverage in Vogue magazine will secure unceasing exposure in future issues. Always remember your competition, press politics and readers needs and try not to grow presumptuous. No designer is thoroughly irresistible to every stylist and just because you have received one piece of fabulous press coverage, you should not automatically assume you have made it. As with any business, you are only as good as your last success and you must try to retain a humble mind as well as a determined attitude.

Computer Un-Friendly

Almost every area of your PR strategy will involve a computer at some point. It is easy to assume that everyone is computer friendly however there will always be a group of people who fear the internet. Computer skills are a must, unless of course your budget allows you to hire reliable and experienced assistants to do the work for you. Even so, do you really want to remain in the dark when emails are sent, press releases posted and accounts organized? By investing a little time and money in to a short course, you could soon find yourself designing, typing and printing everything that is sent out on behalf of your label. From letterheads and basic logo's, to eye catching lookbooks and unique stickers, you and your computer could eliminate printing and professional editing costs altogether. It may not be the easiest of learning curves but it will pay off. Visit your local council office, local library or organisations such as Business Link to discover what courses are available to you.

Common Courtesy

Being courteous will get you far in life and the fashion industry should be no exception to the rules. Just because you confirmed a piece of long lead press coverage with a publication in January, it does not mean you need not thank the responsible contact when the coverage finally comes to print in April. A hand written note of thanks or, on receipt of a particularly fabulous piece of press, a gift (perhaps from a previous or current collection) will go a long way.

Common courtesies can go astray in the fashion arena. Deadlines, editorial issues and general office mayhem can end up taking their toll on even the kindest of stylists and journalists. Remember, it is not personal. As always, put yourselves in their shoes: surrounded by deadlines, focused on pleasing some three hundred thousand females each month. Undoubtedly you will need to find yourself some thick skin when handling your own PR.

On the whole the press are great to work with and high pressure jobs aside, they do appreciate that a PR's job does help them do theirs more efficiently. Once you are ensconced in the arena, then fleeting conversations and harsh rejection should subside, evolving into genuine, professional relationships.

Fashion Talk

Throughout this guide and in general conversation with the fashion press, you might encounter fashion and Public Relation jargon that you are unfamiliar with. Here are some examples of industry words and what they mean.

Account Team   An agency PR team assigned to a client.

Advertorial   A paid for advertisement that is highly reflective of 'real' press coverage.

Break down   Description of what is needed for a shoot: items, colour palettes, deadlines, etc.

Byline   A name credit of a journalist or stylist underneath or aside their feature.

Call – in's   Similar to a break down, a journalist is "calling" something in. A phrase suitable to use when contacting press.

Classic   Used when the theme of a shoot is timeless and uninfluenced by fads.

Consumer   The general customer.

Consumer Title   Publication intended for the general reader.

Copy   Written text.

Cuttings	Relaxed term for cut outs of press coverage direct from the publication.
Cuttings Agency	Agency that assumes responsibility for finding, cutting and keeping press coverage on behalf of their client.
Delivery Note	A sheet enclosed with all deliveries and press returns listing all the enclosed items.
Docket	Alternative name for a Delivery Note.
Editor	A person in charge of a magazine or newspaper.
Editorial	An article giving the Editor's opinion on an issue.
Editorial Department	Relating to the department that selects and prepares material for publication.
Fashion Cupboard	A room/cupboard/section of an office within a publication that houses all products sent by PR's and designers. Usually contactable via fashion assistants. There may be more than one cupboard, depending on the size of the fashion department.
Feature	A detailed article of a subject.
Freelancer	Term applied to an individual who is not employed as a full time member of staff.
Gorilla	Relating to low cost, unconventional methods of raising sales/PR.

Headshot	Photograph of an individual, neck upwards.
IPR	Institute of Public Relations.
J'pegs	Images saved as a j'peg on computer.
Keywords	Words extracted from a press release for use in editorial coverage.
Location (on)	Generally applies to a fashion shoot that is held on or at a specific location. Abroad or on a site suitable to the feature, story or theme.
Long Lead	Non immediate press coverage.
Lookbook	A collection of images from your collection.
Main shoot	Generally the leading fashion feature of an issue. Also refers to a fashion shoot that requires models, usually shot on location.
Model Size	Normally sizes 8 to 10 (unless stated). Shoe size normally size 7 (unless stated).
New Face	Refers to new models, recently launched by their agency.
Newsletter	Regular form of communication. Sent to press and/or customers.
News Release	See Press Release
On Trend	Subscribing to the current fashion trends and movements.

The Pocket Guide To Fashion PR

Pick Up	Usually refers to the pick up of samples by a publications courier.
Post Room	A publications' in-house postal room in which couriers pick up and drop off samples.
Press Office	In-house or outsourced function that handle PR enquiries and campaigns.
Press Pack	A collection of brand information, usually including the press release, lookbook, biography, contact details etc.
Press Release	Written recorded communication directed at target press.
Price Brackets	Also known as 'price points', the term usually refers to the average product price limits a publication will feature.
Product Placement	The placing of products via mediums such as TV, film, theatre and music videos.
Readership	The readers of a publication as a group.
Returns	Term used to cover all samples that are being awaited by a designer or label.
Sample	Refers to products that have been sent to press from a PR or designer.
Shoot/shooting	Refers to a photographic shoot, or the process of.
Shots	Images/pictures.

Short lead	Press coverage that can be achieved quickly, e.g. via a daily publication or internet site.
Show card	Laminated card, exhibiting press coverage. A convenient way of exhibiting press coverage.
Signature Piece	Refers to a piece that best exemplifies your labels philosophy and style.
Still Life	An image or collection of images that are shot without a model. Normally shot on a white background.
Stockist	Boutique, department store, retail outlet that stock your label.
Stylist	Person creating an ensemble for and image or shoot.
Supplement	An additional form of editorial – commonly found with weekend editions of newspapers.
Target Audience	The desired recipients of your message.
Target Publications	Publications whose readership profile best relates to your target audience.
Trade Press	Refers to publications that are directly related to a specific profession or industry.
Transeasonal/ Transitional	Garments that bridge the gap between two seasons.

Examples of Press Coverage

There are various forms of press coverage you will be aiming to achieve. Described below are a few examples.

- **Front Page** - Highly desirable, usually obtained by good fortune

- **Main Fashion Pages** - Products featured in the main fashion pages/features of a publication

- **Editorial Coverage** - A feature on you, your brand and/or your products

- **Online Coverage** - Coverage via target relevant websites

- **Supplements** - Your products featured in a seasonal supplements, e.g. summer shoes, fashion week special etc

- **Trade Press** - Press coverage via your relevant trade publications, e.g. footwear/ethical clothing magazines etc

- **Regional Press** - Publication local to your area of residence/business, most commonly newspapers

- **Celebrity Endorsement** - Can be arranged via personal stylists or direct sales with a celebrity (more commonly through a high profile stockist). Notify key press should an image of your product and the celebrity emerge.

Conclusion

You are now equipped with the basic knowledge to commence with a simple in house PR campaign. As you have read through the chapters, I hope you have dispelled any myths or preconceptions you may have held about this aspect of the fashion industry.

Undoubtedly PR can be as competitive as you might have heard and the rumors of air kissing and such can – in many circles – be true. However this guide subscribes to the idea that fashion PR is about successfully raising the profile of a designer or label. It is focused on attracting the highest possible attention from customers and buyers and ultimately greatly attributing to the rounded success of your business.

PR need not have 'luvvie' connotations. You are able to maintain a successful PR strategy without compromising your personal integrity and even without professional training, you can compete against the larger PR firms, brands and designers.

We hope you have enjoyed reading through this guide and continue to refer to various chapters and points as you work through you PR plan.

The Pocket Guide To Fashion PR was designed for those with little or no experience within the field. If you feel you would like to explore the industry further then do contact colleges, universities and course organisers to see what is available to you. Who knows, you may even want to start a fashion PR firm yourself!

If you would like to discuss coaching opportunities or wish to offer feedback on The Pocket Guide To Fashion PR, please email **fashion@pr-eo.co.uk.**

Notes

The Pocket Guide To Fashion PR